THE UNAUTHORIZED BIOGR...

SCOOP!

ISSUE #2

Chloe x Halle

by Jennifer Poux

Grosset & Dunlap

GROSSET & DUNLAP
An Imprint of Penguin Random House LLC, New York

Illustrations by Becky James

Photo credit: cover: Vivien Killilea/Stringer/Getty Images Entertainment/ Getty Images North America

Visit us online at www.penguinrandomhouse.com.

ISBN 9780593222263   10 9 8 7 6 5 4 3 2 1

TABLE OF CONTENTS

....

CHAPTER 1

LOW-KEY FAMOUS

*I*f you're a fan of Chloe x Halle, you gotta know the incredible story of how they were discovered. (More on that later!) But did you know that long before the Bailey sisters were signed by Queen Bey, they'd already met her?

Here's the **SCOOP!** Chloe was just three years old when she was cast as the child version of Beyoncé's character in the 2003 film *The Fighting Temptations.*

Seriously? As Chloe says, it's pretty funny how the universe works, like she was given a sign early on. It was her first movie audition, and she killed it—five hundred other little girls went home disappointed.

Years passed before the Bailey sisters connected with Beyoncé again. In the meantime, they logged countless hours singing their hearts out and winning talent contests. Some people think of Chloe x Halle as overnight sensations. But they've been honing their musical chops since they were seven and five! Even before they were teens, they were experimenting with harmonies, writing lyrics, singing, and jamming together in their living room. The girls uploaded their first cover song to their YouTube channel in 2011, when they were just thirteen and eleven.

Do you know what song it was?

You're right if you guessed it was a Beyoncé song.

"Lots of people had told us, oh, maybe you should sing this person's song and post it. And then, one day, we were at home and we were like, we're kind of bored, let's just do this, let's sing this song that we like, 'Best Thing I Never Had' by Beyoncé," Halle told ABC News.

The girls found the instrumental version of the song online and recorded it in their basement. Their sister Ski (say: SKY) shot the video. Dad didn't want them to post it on YouTube, but they won him over. In the first few days, the video got a hundred views. The sisters were thrilled! But then, a week or so later, it was up to a mind-blowing ten thousand views! They didn't know what was happening.

You can still catch their version of "Best Thing I Never Had" on the Chloe x Halle YouTube channel. The girls are adorable, wearing red tank tops and big smiles as they introduce themselves to the camera. Then they start to sing. Their voices are more than adorable. They are soulful, power-ful, and extraordinary! The sisters, still so young, already exude cool confidence in front of the camera.

Pretty soon, the phone was blowing up. Chloe

says they were shopping in the supermarket when their father got a call inviting them on *The Ellen DeGeneres Show.* The girls freaked out right in the middle of the store! Wouldn't you?

They performed "Best Thing I Never Had" on *Ellen,* and after that, they were full-fledged YouTube sensations.

Although the girls' early low-key fame came from covers, they had already started writing music. Halle admits their earliest songs were embarrassing. But their father gave them some lessons in the art of songwriting. And he told them they would have more power if they wrote their own music.

"When we were ten and eight years old, our dad sat us down and taught us basic song structure. He's always been an amazing writer. He writes the best poems and the best birthday cards," Halle said on the radio show *Sway's Universe.* He told them to just write about their feelings.

Chloe says their parents never pushed them into the music business—but they were super

SCOOP! FACT:

Mr. Bailey is apparently tone-deaf, but Mrs. Bailey likes to sing in the shower!

supportive. "I'm really grateful, because we have really awesome parents, 'cause they saw that passion and fire in our eyes and how we lit up whenever we did music or entertaining or any type of thing like that," Chloe told the hosts of *The Breakfast Club* radio show.

Mr. and Mrs. Bailey recognized something special in their daughters, and they weren't the only ones. Over the next couple of years, the sisters would rack up more successes, including some minor acting roles. And then, in 2012, they won season five of Radio Disney's *The Next Big Thing*!

Radio Disney said the girls' musical talents and relatable personalities won the hearts of the show's audience. It's that winning combination of their soulful vocals and upbeat, likable personalities that catapulted them into the limelight and kept them there. Their positivity shines through whether they're on a stage singing or playing twins in the TV show *Grown-ish*. Call it the "it factor."

And there's something else, too. It's the something that makes their harmonies so hauntingly beautiful and their vibe so chill.

They're sisters. The more you learn about Chloe and Halle, the more you'll understand the power of their bond. Interviewers often mistake them for twins, and it's easy to see why: They have a relationship that's unique, even for siblings, and their connection resonates throughout the story of their young lives.

CHAPTER 2

FAMILY SECRETS

*B*efore they stylized their names as Chloe x Halle, they were just Chloe and Halle Bailey of Atlanta, Georgia. The girls lived there with their parents, Courtney and Doug Bailey; their older sister, Ski; and their younger brother, Branson—one big happy family. Dad was a stockbroker before he became the girls' full-time manager. Their mom worked in human resources.

Chloe was born July 1, 1998, under the astrological sign Cancer. Cancer's ruling element is water, and Chloe is drawn to water because it makes her feel spiritually cleansed. People born under this sign tend to be fiercely loyal and family-oriented. Makes sense. Chloe is totally devoted to her parents and her siblings, especially Halle. She's the ultimate big sister!

Halle was born March 27, 2000, which makes her an Aries. Her element is fire, and yes, the girl is on fire! Not to mention, people born under this sign are super creative. Check. Aries women are also supposed to have an awesome sense of style. Check, check. If you've seen any of Chloe x Halle's appearances, you know that's true! (More on that later.)

SCOOP! FACT

Even though Chloe was born first, she says her sister sometimes acts like the older one. And she calls her "an old soul."

The Baileys moved to Los Angeles when the girls were still pretty young to be closer to the music scene.

"The last day we were packing at our house [in Atlanta] we saw this huge grasshopper on the door. And we're super into symbolisms, and what the universe is trying to tell us, and we looked it up and it was like, leap forward, you're going in the right direction," Chloe said on the *Sway's Universe* radio show.

To move their careers in the right direction, the sisters were homeschooled starting in seventh and fifth grade. That gave them time to go to auditions and work on their music. Chloe says that's when they really got tight.

"Before that we were like, okay, yeah, we're sisters, but once we realized we were really all we had, we got so, so close. And I feel like we're twins, even though we're not. We're so in sync," Chloe said when the sisters talked about their relationship on *Sway's Universe*.

Halle says Chloe continues to be her inspiration. "I look to her as my role model and the person I just always want to be with all the time, and you know when one is down, we lift the other one up." Serious sister goals!

But, come on—are they for real? Don't they ever fight?

Once in a while, of course! They say it's always

about small stuff, like clothes. But they claim they never stay angry with each other for long.

And here's a shocker: Halle says they are complete opposites! That they balance each other out. It's true that Chloe is more bubbly and talkative in interviews—often taking the lead. Maybe that's because she's the oldest. But it's also because she's naturally outgoing. Halle tends to be a little calmer, quieter. She calls herself a homebody. But, surprisingly, when asked who's more of a diva, the sisters agree that Halle wears that crown.

When Chloe and Halle have time to chill, they're into hiking, going to the beach, and vision boarding. The walls of their bedrooms and home studio are collages of pictures and inspirational words they've clipped and collected—all their aspirational goals for the future.

"It's things that we'd like to speak into existence or for our life to be like," Chloe told *Vulture*. Words like *dangerous* and *heroes* have spent time on their walls.

They're also binge-watchers—intense series like *Game of Thrones*, *The Handmaid's Tale*, and *Black Mirror* are in the Bailey queue. They both like to read, too. Chloe's into self-help books and thrillers. Halle gravitates toward American literature, particularly poets like Langston Hughes.

Even though they were initially homeschooled, both girls graduated from a traditional high school. After tenth grade, Chloe got her GED and went to prom with a friend. Halle graduated in 2018. Did she go to prom? Nope. But don't feel too sorry for her: It was the weekend of Coachella, and Chloe x Halle were performing! (Prom or Coachella? Hmm . . .) That's a pretty awesome trade-off.

Despite their busy schedules, Chloe learned to drive and got her license in LA. It took a while— she found driving pretty scary and let her learner's permit lapse before she finally went for it. (Driving in LA is not for the faint of heart.) She drives a Mini Cooper that's blue, her favorite color. No license for Halle yet, but luckily, she has her big sister to chauffeur her around.

On the road or at home, both Chloe and Halle are committed vegans. And here are the deets: They went vegetarian years ago when their mom wanted to try it. But even after their mother returned to the carnivore life, the girls never looked back. And a few years ago, they went full vegan, which they say is easy to do in LA, with so many vegan-friendly restaurants and fresh produce all year. But don't think that means they always eat healthy. They love their snacks and junk food like everybody else. And Chloe says she still loves carbs and is even known to order in spaghetti from room service.

So . . . by now you're probably wondering about their love lives.

Here's the SCOOP! According to Chloe and Halle, they really don't have time for relationships right now. Hmmm . . . really?

They insist they're working too hard and they're too focused to get distracted by dating. Halle says neither of them has had their heart broken yet. So how do they write songs about things they've never been through, songs like "Happy Without Me"? They use their imaginations. Halle says if they wrote only about what they know, their songs would all be about working hard!

They might not be in love, but they get star-struck like the rest of us. Halle adores the musician Lenny Kravitz—whom she's met a few times—especially because she admires his guitar skills. And Chloe was practically tongue-tied when she met actor/singer/writer Donald Glover. They were also starstruck when they met Michelle Obama—twice! She introduced them at the White House Easter Egg Roll and at the South by Southwest festival. What was that like?

"Oh my goodness. You get goose bumps just even saying her name," Chloe said during an interview on ABC's *Nightline*. "I remember we were backstage, and we were about to go on, and I was just overwhelmed with happiness, and I was about to break down crying before we went on while she was introducing us."

Once upon a time, they would have been tongue-tied in the presence of the queen of music royalty—you know, Beyoncé. But that was a lifetime ago. Now, Beyoncé is their mentor and friend.

Can you even IMAGINE???

ON ONE OF ATLANTA'S MOST INFLUENTIAL PEOPLE: MARTIN LUTHER KING JR.

Born in Atlanta, Georgia, on January 15, 1929, Martin Luther King Jr. was an American activist, minister, and leader in the civil rights movement from 1955 until his assassination in 1968. He is best known for advancing civil rights through nonviolence and civil disobedience.

On August 28, 1963, King helped lead the March on Washington, at which he delivered his famous seventeen-minute "I Have a Dream" speech to an estimated 250,000 people.

The march was one of the largest political rallies for human rights in United States history and is credited with helping pass the Civil Rights Act of 1964.

More Sister Goals

Before there was Chloe x Halle, these sisters made big names for themselves—some together, some separately.

1. Beyoncé and Solange Knowles
2. Venus and Serena Williams
3. Dakota and Elle Fanning
4. Jessica and Ashlee Simpson
5. Mary-Kate and Ashley Olsen
6. Malia and Sasha Obama
7. Kylie and Kendall Jenner
8. Tia and Tamera Mowry
9. Gigi and Bella Hadid
10. Hilary and Haylie Duff

SCOOP! QUIZ

WHO SAID IT?

How well do you know Chloe and Halle as individuals?

↓ MATCH THE QUOTE ↓
WITH THE SPEAKER.

See page 94 for answers.

1

"I'm just really grateful for this time. I feel like I'm figuring out who I truly am as a human being, as well as an artist."

2

"We think it's so cool when people are dancing to our music—that's just such a wonderful sight to see."

3 "I learned how to drive there [LA]. I feel like if I can drive there, I can drive anywhere."

4 "I love poems, and Langston Hughes is somebody who is always amazing."

5 "I love wearing flowy stuff because it feels like I can just move around everywhere and at the same time be pretty. It's a bit more boho."

6 "I really love looking for bomber jackets and platform boots and sneakers because you can always throw them on and elevate your look."

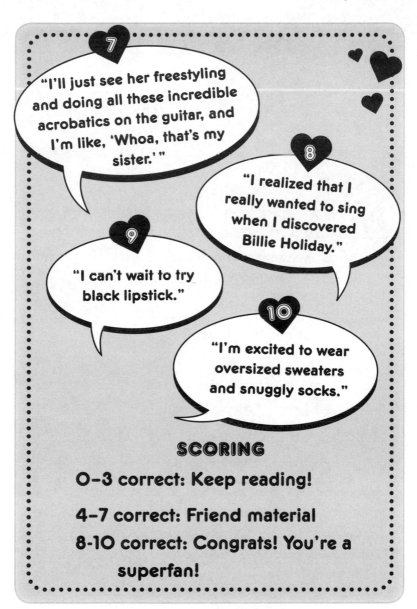

7 "I'll just see her freestyling and doing all these incredible acrobatics on the guitar, and I'm like, 'Whoa, that's my sister.'"

8 "I realized that I really wanted to sing when I discovered Billie Holiday."

9 "I can't wait to try black lipstick."

10 "I'm excited to wear oversized sweaters and snuggly socks."

SCORING

0–3 correct: Keep reading!

4–7 correct: Friend material

8-10 correct: Congrats! You're a superfan!

CHAPTER 3

ENTER QUEEN BEY

In December of 2013, Chloe and Halle uploaded a video to YouTube. The girls stood in front of a wooden door wearing baseball-style T-shirts—their only adornment was thirteen-year-old Halle's sparkly silver headband. (Too cute!) They both sang, and Chloe played piano.

They didn't think that video would change their lives. They just wanted to record another Beyoncé song they liked, "Pretty Hurts."

Here's an impressive stat: That video now has nearly eighteen million views!

The "Pretty Hurts" video gained traction from the start, getting more views than their videos usually did. It is a truly soulful rendition of the song, and it's easy to see why people liked it and shared it.

Here's the SCOOP! The views kept ticking up, and then one VIP watched. One day out of the blue, the Baileys received an email from Parkwood Entertainment, asking if Beyoncé could post the video on her social media platforms. And, the email asked, did the girls have representation?

The Bailey family responded that of course she could post their videos, and no, the girls weren't signed with anyone yet. (The family had turned down a number of record deals they didn't like.) A few days later, Beyoncé said she wanted to sign them with her entertainment management company!

"We were flipping out!" Chloe said in an interview with Hot 97's Nessa. "We were losing our marbles!" Halle said.

In so many of the interviews with Chloe and Halle on TV and radio stations and in print, the sisters are often asked about that story. Interviewers usually say something like "Is it really true that Beyoncé discovered you on YouTube?" It's almost as if they just can't believe it, like it's an urban legend. It sounds too good to be true, don't you think?

But it is 100 percent true. Chloe says it was shocking for them!

After all, think of the huge number of people out there who have uploaded their music videos to YouTube. Some of them aren't so good—some of them are amazing. But most of them never have this kind of success, even if they go viral. It was beyond the Baileys' wildest dreams.

Pretty soon the girls were sending some of the songs they had written to Beyoncé for critique. (Imagine waiting on that feedback!) But it was all

SCOOP! FACT

Beyoncé didn't realize Chloe was the girl who played her in *The Fighting Temptations*.

good. Queen Bey sent them notes, telling them what she loved and offering advice on how to improve some of their songs.

Chloe and Halle say because Beyoncé had gone through everything they were now experiencing, she was helpful with advice in all spheres of their lives, and truly supportive. And she didn't try to change them.

"I love her so much because she allows us to shine as individual beings," Chloe said in a *Breakfast Club* radio interview. "And she knows how powerful she is, and she's lending us her resources but also letting us shine on our own. And I think that's something pretty special because, you know, a lot of artists, they'll sign to these big labels and they'll be taught what to wear and how to sing and how to move and all that, but we get to create what we want to create. And, of course, we'll send her songs and she'll give us her notes, but at the end of the day she's always like, we get to do what we want to do and, you know, don't dumb yourself down for the world. Let the world catch up to you."

Chloe knows the score: It doesn't always go that way. Some artist management companies and record labels are super controlling—they'll transform the artist into something very different than she was before she was discovered. So far, the sisters have been able to record their own material and retain their look and image, including their beautiful dreadlocks. (Apparently, in the past, some talent agents told them to nix their dreads.)

Now Chloe x Halle often work with big-time record producers and artists, recording in professional studios, which is very cool. But they've learned from their royal mentor to believe in the music they write and produce themselves. They still love to make music at home.

"It's an incredible feeling, because yes, we do believe in ourselves, but hearing that from Beyoncé makes us believe in ourselves even more," Chloe said in an interview with *Paper Magazine*.

It's been a whirlwind of activity since Queen

Bey took Chloe and Halle under her wing. They've had concert tours, a White House visit, album releases, and a Super Bowl performance, just to name a few. Beyoncé has been like a fairy godmother, helping the Bailey sisters live out their dreams.

SCOOP! QUIZ

HOW WELL DO YOU KNOW BEYONCÉ?

Take our quiz to find out if you're in the Know(les)! See page 94 for answers.

1. What's Beyoncé's middle name?

2. Where was Beyoncé born?

3. What was the name of her group before she went solo?

4. What's the title of her first solo album?

5. What Beyoncé album became the best-selling album of 2016?

6. Who's Beyoncé's famous sister?

7. What's the full name of Beyoncé and Jay-Z's first child?

8. What are the first names of their twins?

9. Who's Beyoncé's alter ego?

10. Who did Beyoncé play in the new *Lion King* movie?

SCORING

1–4 correct answers: You're no bae to Bey

5–7 correct answers: Don't expect a dinner invite to the Carters' house

8–10 correct answers: Congrats! You're in the Know(les)!

CHAPTER 4

A FAIRY-TALE LIFE

*H*ow do you top singing with Beyoncé? That's easy. Appear in videos on her celebrated visual album, *Lemonade*, which dropped in the spring of 2016.

The sisters show up in the video's Resurrection section. And in that iconic photo: on a stoop in Louisiana, with actresses Amandla Stenberg and Zendaya, and Lisa Kaindé-Diaz and Naomi Diaz of the twin-sister singing duo Ibeyi. And, of course, Beyoncé. It's a visual symbol of black female empowerment and beauty, and the two young Bailey sisters are positioned to be its future.

"Just being in the midst of 'black girl magic' was amazing," Halle told *Vulture*. (Can you imagine?)

Less than a week after *Lemonade* was released,

Chloe x Halle dropped their own *Sugar Symphony* EP. (Coincidence? Hardly.) It was a heady time. The sisters got to sing the national anthem at the BET Experience. And if all that wasn't enough, they traveled through Europe that summer, opening for Beyoncé's Formation World Tour. Did you catch that? They were the opening act for huge crowds of Beyoncé fans, in gigantic stadiums!

Even before *Lemonade* became THE album, Chloe x Halle would meet another icon, one of their heroes. Chloe x Halle opened for Michelle Obama's keynote speech at South by Southwest that year. Introduced to the sisters by her own daughters, Malia and Sasha, the First Lady gave them serious props in her intro. And then, because she was apparently so taken with them, the First

SCOOP! FACT

Lemonade was the best-selling album of 2016, with 2.5 million copies sold. It won two Grammy Awards: one for Best Urban Contemporary Album and one for Best Music Video.

Lady added them to the White House Easter Egg Roll, where they were the opening act. (You sensing a theme here?) Beyoncé and Blue Ivy were on the White House lawn for that one. The weekend was also Halle's sixteenth birthday. (Learn to drive? Or sing at the White House? Hmmm . . .)

"Greatest sixteenth birthday ever!" Halle told *Vulture*. No kidding.

Then, two years after the Formation tour, following the release of their *The Kids Are Alright* debut album (more on that later!), their fairy godmother and her husband, Jay-Z, took the girls on the bus again, this time on the North American leg of their On the Run II Tour, with DJ Khaled. And, once again, they would be the opening act! (Guess they did pretty well the first time.)

"It's really cool, because we're learning so much, and we get to watch her [Beyoncé] every night give 150 percent," Halle said during the tour, in an interview with radio personality Nessa on Hot 97. And they got to hang out with the Carters during the day.

Chloe says on the road, they're always learning and growing.

"So many souls out in the audience—you want to connect with each and every one of them. I feel like every time we go out there, we're just getting a step ahead [from] where we were the day before."

Does it get lonely on the road?

"For me, I have my sister. I'm the little sister, so as long as she's here, I'm good," said Chloe. (How many times can you say "sister goals" in one book?)

They didn't stay on the road forever. They made it home in time for Thanksgiving and Christmas, and then it was off to Super Bowl LIII, where they sang "America the Beautiful," in the city of their birth, Atlanta. What a thrill!

All that in a few years, and that doesn't include the many other amazing things that have happened to Chloe and Halle Bailey—the TV roles, the fashion shows, the album release. That's all coming up.

ON THE WHITE HOUSE EASTER EGG ROLL

The White House Easter Egg Roll tradition dates all the way back to 1878 under the administration of the nineteenth president, Rutherford B. Hayes.

That year, children showed up to the White House front gate, hoping to be able to roll their toy eggs on the lawn. Much to their surprise, President Hayes allowed them to do so! And thus began the annual tradition.

Because of World War I and II, there were no egg rolls from 1917 to 1920 and from 1943 to 1945.

Following World War II, the White House underwent years of construction. It wasn't until President Dwight D. Eisenhower reinstated the tradition in 1953 that children were once again rolling eggs on the lawn!

SCOOP! EXTRA

WORDS FROM THE WISE:
INSPIRATION FROM CHLOE AND HALLE

Here are some of Chloe x Halle's most inspirational quotes to get you up and running.

1 "You know, I really don't care if I'm progressing in music life or acting life—if I'm just happy, I'm good. That's, like, the first thing, really. And, of course, I want to grow every day as a person. But all of this stuff, the glitz and the glam and stuff, I mean it's wonderful, but that's not so important to me."—Halle

2 "The only thing I fear is not taking risks and not being completely who I am. And I'm so glad my sister and I are here together to just keep each other on the right path and just always do what's right and what's positive."—Chloe

3 "Don't be afraid—you're magical. You hold so much power in your hands."—Halle

4 "Just believe in yourself. Because when you believe in yourself, the outside does not matter. Don't let anybody tell you you cannot do something. Because you can, and you should prove them wrong, because that is the most fun thing, when you can turn around and be like, 'Ha, I did it. Okay.' "—Chloe

5 "You should just be confident in the skin you're in, and everyone is beautiful no matter what shade." —Chloe

6 "Block out the naysayers and just keep doing what's meant for you."—Halle

7 "You always want to be better tomorrow than you were today. And what we realize is the more hard work we put into it, all of these blessings come out of that. When you find something that you love and you're passionate about, it doesn't really feel like work."—Chloe

8 "Even if we didn't have people who loved our music, I would still be content and happy in what I'm doing, because it's what I love."—Halle

CHAPTER 5

SOULS ON FIRE

Chloe and Halle are deeply passionate about their music. They give off that vibe in every performance—there's no faking that kind of commitment. And even though they're now TV stars on *Grown-ish*, they both call music their first love.

Chloe says music "lights [their] souls on fire." (You gotta love the poetry.) That's why the sisters throw themselves into writing, producing, and singing. As Chloe says, it's not a job when you love it. That passion propels them to improve at their instruments—Chloe plays piano and Halle plays guitar—and it's what pushes them toward excellence in their craft, which is always evolving depending on what's happening in their lives and who they're listening to. Halle even named her acoustic guitar! She calls it "Soul."

Both of the Baileys say their musical tastes are all over the place. They're inspired by everything from jazz to Rihanna to Frank Ocean to Coldplay. Halle has long been enamored with Billie Holiday, a jazz singer who had a twenty-five-year career long ago. Lady Day was known for her silky vocals and unusual stylings. (Sound familiar?) Halle says she first saw her on the pink cover of a CD (a Billie Holiday compilation) with a rose in her hair. Halle was a little girl, and it made a big impression on her. Then she listened to Billie sing, and she was blown away. She's been listening to her and jazz artists like Sarah Vaughan ever since.

For years, Chloe and Halle produced all of their music in their living room, and they still work in their home studio whenever they can. (Yes, they have one, right next to the living room.) Halle says her sister never gives herself enough credit, that Chloe is really the producer. She gives her major props for her skills! But they both write their songs. And they're always open to checking out new sounds.

"We just kind of love to experiment, throw things out and see what sticks," Chloe said in an interview on *The Breakfast Club* radio show. "We're more of, like, the feeling type of girls. And if we don't know something, we look it up. I guess we grew up having that 'if you don't know, figure it out' mentality from our parents."

Here's the SCOOP! Chloe and Halle literally taught themselves how to record and produce songs.

Seriously! There were no classes, no producers coming over to teach them. Chloe says they use Logic Pro X and Ableton software. They've watched tons of tutorials on the Internet to learn how to use the software and make their magic happen. Even now, when they don't know how

SCOOP! FACT

Beyoncé likes to call them her "little aliens" for their sharp musical instincts.

to do something, they just google it.

And they incorporate a wide range of music genres and styles into their songs, which makes it difficult to slap a label on them. You'll hear R&B, rock, pop, gospel, jazz, classical—even some musical theater—in their music. Whatever the genre, their songs get stuck in your head. Even though they're so young, their songs aren't just for kids. They have plenty of adult fans.

After Beyoncé came into their lives, Chloe x Halle made their first EP, which they produced in that home studio. It was released by Parkwood and Columbia Records in April 2016. EP stands for *extended play*, which is more material than a single and shorter than an album. An EP usually has four to six tracks on it. Their EP, *Sugar Symphony*, has five.

The first song on *Sugar Symphony*, called "Drop,"

has a haunting and hypnotic vibe. Nothing basic about it. "Drop" doesn't sound like a typical pop song, except, maybe, for the lyrics. You might listen to it and think it's about a relationship gone bad.

> "Baby I get sick of you.
> You're the same old tune.
> I don't ever want to hear you again."
>
> ◄◄ ❚❚ ►►

Here's another SCOOP! "Drop" is actually about a song! Listen again and you'll get it. The sisters say they were inspired to write "Drop" after spending so much time on another song that they were totally over it.

According to *Rolling Stone* magazine, when Beyoncé heard "Drop" she called the Bailey sisters and said, "Oh my gosh, girls, this is amazing. You guys are so talented. Your head is in the right direction."

The rest of the EP is equally cool. The vocals

in "Fall" are so clear, and, at times, this track sounds classical. "Lazy Love" sounds more like a pop song than the other tracks. "Thunder" has an old-fashioned vibe with a modern twist. Chloe x Halle teamed up with Hit-Boy (so cool) to write "Red Lights."

If you had to come up with a one-word description of *Sugar Symphony*, it might be *moody*. It's a little dark, in a good way. Each track is unexpected—the beats, the turns they take. And, as always, the vocals are crazy-good. Some critics say they have the voices of angels. (But do angels have so much power?)

Speaking of power, in addition to singing, Halle loves guitar. She calls herself an amateur, but Chloe says no way—she's a pro. She says it's amazing to see what her sister can do with a guitar. Asked what she would do if she could only have an acoustic or an electric, Halle would choose electric because she really wants to be able to shred. That would be epic!

No matter what the Bailey sisters do, they slay. And it's not by accident, or luck. Sure, they've had some of that. But these women never stop working. They're constantly upping their game. They may be young, but they've been preparing for this most of their lives.

Now, you could say they're adulting. And the hard work is paying off in a big way. But the payoff is more than fame and money. (Is there more, you ask?)

"Music is definitely my outlet," Chloe said on *The Breakfast Club* radio show. "I feel like we're all born with a gift, and it's your job to share it and inspire others."

There's no question they've inspired millions of people. And, thankfully, they keep on sharing . . . and growing.

HERE'S THE SCOOP!

. . . ON JAZZ. DIG THIS!

Jazz music traces its roots back to African American communities in New Orleans, Louisiana, during the late nineteenth and early twentieth centuries.

While jazz music is often difficult to define, the music grew out of traditional blues and ragtime. Jazz legends like trumpeter Louis Armstrong and pianist Duke Ellington played these traditional songs, but relied heavily on improvisation while playing.

As a result, improvisation became one of the defining qualities of the genre that is difficult to define!

The 1920s are referred to as "the Jazz Age" because jazz was the major form of musical expression.

CHAPTER 6

TV TWINS

> Watch out, world, I'm grown now
> It's about to go down
> My heart beatin' so loud
> Mama, look, I'm grown now (I'm grown!)
>
> ◄◄ ❚❚ ►►

*T*hat's the first verse of "Grown," the catchy theme to the TV show *Grown-ish*, written by Chloe x Halle for the *Black-ish* spinoff. You gotta check out the video. It might as well be about the sisters, too. And suddenly, they're adults.

Here's the catch: The show's not really about them at all, because A) they play sisters who are twins, B) they don't go to college in real life, and C) they're really different from their characters.

The Baileys play twins Jazlyn and Skyler Forster, track stars at the fictitious California University, and friends to Zoey Johnson, the show's main

47

character. They curse, and drink at parties, and have boyfriends—stuff that (apparently) is foreign to Chloe and Halle.

The stories on *Grown-ish* are edgy and contemporary. If you haven't seen it, *Grown-ish* is all about college life, and anything goes. The show deals with drug and alcohol use, sex, relationship goals, betrayal, issues of race, control over your own body, and girl power. It's about what happens when you leave home and have to figure things out for yourself. And it's all from the perspective of Zoey, the oldest kid in the Johnson household in *Black-ish*. Played by Yara Shahidi, she's beautiful, privileged, and totally stylin'. All the kids are, a little unrealistically so. (How many college students wear head-to-toe Gucci?) But it's fun to check out their ever-changing outfits and Zoey's wigs.

Zoey breaks the fourth wall—meaning she addresses the audience. And she lets you in on her real feelings and her problems, like her boyfriend, played in season two by Luka Sabbat. He's super chill—she, not so much. Her friend group is diverse and gets real with each other most of the time. The twins always speak their minds when they offer advice.

How'd they get the gig?

Here's the SCOOP! Chloe says they accepted an award for Beyoncé at the BET Awards a few years ago. Yara Shahidi, a friend of the sisters, presented the award. Kenya Barris, creator of _Black-ish_ and one of the creators of _Grown-ish_, saw the three girls together onstage and invited the Baileys to his office.

Chloe says it was good vibes from the start.

"And next thing you know, he was like, 'I'd love for you guys to be on this show.' We were like, of course, and we didn't even really audition for it," Chloe told _The Breakfast Club_ radio show. "And

I remember the very first time we went into a table read and we saw the script, and before this show, we didn't really cuss like that, but it was fun because our characters, Jazlyn and Skyler, they're like the complete opposite of us, and . . . we bring out our inner Atlanta."

SCOOP! FACT

In interviews (and, apparently, in life in general) Chloe and Halle never curse, and they say "Oh my gosh!" instead of "God." So, Chloe adds that it's liberating to be able to "cuss" on TV.

Halle says it's really fun to play Jaz and Sky because they're sassy and "attitude-y." She admits she can also be like that (diva, remember?), but it's fun to bring out that side of her in full on the show. The characters present to the world that they're all lightness and politeness, but with their friends, they're "ratchet," as she says.

There's a lot of commentary on people being "basic" on the show, which is not considered a good thing. The twins are anything but. All the women are independent and doing something interesting. And they have each other's back when things get real. They give each other props when deserved. Some of their behavior isn't exactly stellar, to say the least, but overall, they tend to be aspirational for young women going off to college.

Do Chloe and Halle think they'll ever go to college? They both would like to. They think it would be a great growth experience. But right now, life is too busy and it's taking them on a different path. Halle often says God has a path for them, and they're where they're supposed to be.

Season two is out now, and the show has been picked up for a third season. Are the sisters getting too busy for it? They say no! They love *Grown-ish*, and they're totally on board. Halle says a lot of their friendships are with cast members.

Chloe and Halle are somehow able to star in a TV show, tour with the Carters, and record their first major album. They're wonder women, and still, they're just kids.

SCOOP! QUIZ

WHO'S WHO?

Maybe you do, maybe you don't watch *Grownish* yet. But can you match the characters with the actors who play them? See page 94 for answers.

1. Zoey Johnson	**Trevor Jackson**
2. Luca	**Chloe Bailey**
3. Jazlyn Forster	**Yara Shahidi**
4. Nomi Segal	**Francia Raisa**
5. Aaron Jackson	**Jordan Buhat**
6. Skyler Forster	**Halle Bailey**
7. Ana Torres	**Emily Arlook**
8. Vivek Shah	**Luka Sabbat**

CHAPTER 7

THE KIDS ARE (MORE THAN) ALRIGHT

*W*hen it came time for Chloe x Halle to make their debut studio album, it didn't just pop up overnight. Chloe says they worked on it for about three years, releasing it in the spring of 2018. And this stat will blow your mind: They had to choose the tracks from a catalog of more than FOUR HUNDRED songs they had written over the years! Whoa.

"We think of all our songs as our babies, so it's really hard to choose. That's why the mixtape [*The Two of Us*], we put it out there as the album rejects—but we still love those songs. Working on the album, it took a lot of preciseness to figure out what we wanted to include. We feel like this album is our baby," Halle told *TIME* magazine when the album was released.

An eighteen-song baby! And though some of the songs are collaborations with other artists, the sisters earned songwriting credit on every track. Chloe is the producer on all but three of them. That's phenomenal.

They decided to name the album *The Kids Are Alright*, a title that reflects where they were in their lives: kids growing into adults, doing okay, making some mistakes but learning along the way and being better for it. (They're more than all right.) But it's also a title that speaks to a new generation.

"Being a part of Generation Z, there's a lot of underestimation, and there's so many crazy things happening in the world, and everyone's wondering if we'll be okay," Chloe said in a *Sway's Universe* radio interview. "Even sometimes, I'm like, will we be okay? But I'm like, the kids today, we learn how to take negativity and turn it into something positive, whether it's through our voices or our art or even online and in protesting and in doing the marches and all of that good stuff. And that title just means so much to us."

The Bailey sisters don't get political in these songs or during their interviews. But that doesn't mean they aren't opinionated. And, clearly, they respect those in their generation who are political.

In the title track, they tell their young listeners to go for it! You don't have to wait until you're an adult to make the change you want to see, or do your art.

Do it while you young
Don't let them turn you numb
Don't let them get you strung
Ooh let me put you on
Don't listen to them lies
Stop following the hype
Better meditate, better namaste
Better go and get your life

Talk about practicing what you preach. Nobody could ever accuse them of not going for it.

Some of the album's tracks, like "Drop" and "Fall," were also on *Sugar Symphony*. The album includes "Grown," the fun theme from *Grown-ish*, and "Warrior" from the movie *A Wrinkle in Time*. And it includes one of their most gorgeous songs: "Cool People." It's a showcase for their vocals— Chloe's velvety R&B sound, Halle's satiny jazz style—and their perfect harmonies. And it's catchy. Listen a couple of times and you won't be able to get the tune or the lyrics out of your head.

> I've been down on the regular
> I've seen things with my retina
> These old days I don't feel that much
>
> But darling when you smile it's like the
>   rain dries out
> Now there's no more room for clouds
> Got me singing Hallelu, oh Hallelu oh
> When you hold my hand it just reminds
>   me how
> There's still cool people in the world

And check out appearances by rappers GoldLink, Joey Bada$$, and Kari Faux.

The album received stellar reviews. One

reviewer for *Pitchfork* called it fearless, saying it is "reshaping pop and R&B in their own images," a pitch-perfect commentary.

So many of the songs are unfamiliar—their structures aren't typical or predictable. They can't easily be classified. And, as always, their harmonies are heavenly.

One of the album's tracks speaks to the sisters' strong belief in God. They were raised as nondenominational Christians.

"We've always been into God," Halle said during their *Sway's Universe* radio interview. "That has been our staple since we were little girls. And we believe in manifesting positivity into your life, you know, just with being happy and being a great person in general."

The girls say God is with them through everything—he's their best friend.

Chloe says when she first heard the lyrics to "If God Spoke," written by Halle, she thought they were beautiful. When she asked Halle what they meant, her sister said that it's what God might say if it were talking to them.

Here's the SCOOP! You might think it's a little strange that sometimes they refer to God as "it," but they believe that God is light, and "it" could be male or female, that God is inside everyone.

The Bailey sisters can get deep and philosophical, but they also love to have fun, and they always do it in style.

NAME GAMES

This is not the first record album titled *The Kids Are Alright* and probably won't be the last. The Who, a rock band from England that got its start in the 1960s and still plays today, made an album called *The Kids Are Alright*, a companion to a documentary about the band that has the same name. That record was released on vinyl in 1979, nearly forty years before Chloe x Halle's album. In 2010, there was also another film called *The Kids Are All Right*, starring Julianne Moore, Annette Bening, Mark Ruffalo, Josh Hutcherson, and Mia Wasikowska. And there was a TV sitcom called *The Kids Are Alright* on ABC that lasted just one season, in 2018.

SCOOP! QUIZ

HOW WELL DO YOU KNOW THE ALBUM?

Do you think you know the album inside and out? Match the lyrics with the song title.

1. I can't sleep, I'm wide awake
   I've been up since yesterday

2. She was raised right
   Even when the world is on
     her shoulders
   She'll remain refined
   Like a diamond she'll keep
     shinin'

3. Sometimes I talk to myself,
     self, self, self

4. I've been down on the regular
   I've seen things with my retina

5. I remember when you yelled at
     me, oh
   Cursed my name and then you
     stomped your feet, oh

6. Baby I get sick of you
   You're that same old tune
   I don't ever wanna hear you
     again

7. If I'm in the mood I get as
     ratchet as I wanna
   Turn around and show you,
   I could bless you with some
     culture

8. And I remember you would
     hold my hand
   And call me baby while we
     dancing in the parking lot
     so slow

IF GOD SPOKE

COOL PEOPLE

GROWN

DROP

FAKE

THE KIDS ARE ALRIGHT

HAPPY WITHOUT ME

HELLO FRIEND

SCORING:

1–4 correct answers: Time to put your records on

5–7 correct answers: You're all right

8–10 correct answers: Grammy-worthy!

CHAPTER 8

STYLE ICONS

We don't really care about the trends you like to follow."

The sisters are trendsetters, not followers, as they sing in the title track of *The Kids Are Alright*. It hasn't always been that way. Remember those cute baseball T-shirts and the silver headband? Gone. Chloe x Halle have traversed many a red carpet since those early days in yoga pants. Although the yoga pants make sense since the sisters practice "hot" yoga regularly. Every year, it seems, their fashion evolves, becomes more adventurous and sophisticated. Whenever they hit the stage, the runway, or the screen, they are fire!

There are two constants over the years:

1. Their hair is always natural and usually worn

in dreadlocks. (More on that later!)

2. Their stage and recording outfits are coordinated but never matchy-matchy. They might be cut from the same cloth, but the style is different, or the colors are the same but everything else is different. They always bring it with their individuality. You'll see more short dresses on Halle, gowns on Chloe. Gargantuan, bejeweled earrings on both.

In the early days, their mother would pull together their performance outfits. Sweet, youthful dresses in the same colors. Now they have a stylist, Zerina Akers, who also styles Beyoncé (not a coincidence), Ava DuVernay, and Yara Shahidi. But that doesn't mean they don't put their own super-cool stamp on their clothes.

Their style runs from comfortable color-blocked knits to costume-y—huge shoulders, wild patterns, metallics. (A little Gaga, or even Bowie.) Often, it's straight-up couture glam. As they've gotten older, they've shown more skin, but they're never wildly risqué. (So far, nobody's comparing their fashion choices to Miley's.) And they usually go big on color—bold and fearless.

Check out the Chloe x Halle Instagram (2.2 million followers) for some of their best fashion.

When they're more casual, they go for comfort: Chloe's into sweats and sneakers, hair down. Halle likes things to be a little more flowy, more "boho."

Their shopping styles differ, too. Chloe likes scouring the Melrose Trading Post, a flea market in LA. Halle loves Free People. (Who doesn't?)

And with their always-upward trajectory in the music world, fashion houses have taken note of their fierce style.

The girls made their runway debut in Milan, Italy, in February 2017 for the fashion house Dolce & Gabbana. They were dressed like queens (they are queens!) in black dresses with jeweled gold crowns and all. They say they practiced their catwalk strut in front of any mirror in their sights. (Chloe's got the "head held high" mastered.) And they figured out how to do it by watching Naomi Campbell videos. (Sense a pattern in how they learn?)

They told Vogue.com, "Performing as musicians in front of large audiences made it so much easier to walk in a runway show. When we are singing onstage, most of the time our brains are focusing on what chords to play and what notes to hit, but being a part of the show and only having to walk feels like a breeze, because we're not having to deal with those other factors." (Any models feeling bruised?)

They rocked it and were invited to other shows, and were even front-row guests at Louis Vuitton. They've modeled for Rodarte (one of their faves), and now they have a shoe deal with Teva.

SCOOP! FACT
Rodarte featured Chloe and Halle in its fall 2018 lookbook, along with musicians Grimes and Joanna Newsom.

Teva? Sounds like an unlikely pairing. But it's happening and they're working it, bringing a new vibe to the brand of outdoor sandals that might have been more at home on parents and their young kids before Chloe and Halle came along. (Check out the Indio Jewell and the Ember Moc.)

Teva is all about free-spirited style, as are the Baileys, so it could be a heavenly match.

But if there is one thing that really sets the Baileys' look apart, it's their hair.

Here's the SCOOP! Chloe and Halle have been growing their dreadlocks since they were little girls. It's like their signature look. It's kinda hard to imagine them without their beautiful locs.

Their mom would do their hair when they were kids, or they would do each other's. Although they have professionals now in LA and New York to style them, they still help each other with their dreads and do their own maintenance. And they always keep it natural.

Keeping it natural and going for gorgeous at one of the biggest awards shows out there—that's up next.

GET CHLOE AND HALLE'S STYLE!

The key to Chloe x Halle's style is confidence. Whatever you wear, add a little 'tude!

- ★ **Go natural! Whether your hair is straight, curly, wavy—embrace it! Wear it down for the day, try up at night.**

- ★ **Don't be afraid of color in your clothes! Go bold with bright primary colors like red, blue, and yellow, or purples and magenta, or maybe a little neon and metallics.**

- ★ **Show off your confidence in body-con dresses in fruity colors—peach, green, yellow.**

- ★ **Embrace prints! Floral, stripes, plaid, it's all good.**

★ Get a little edgy with combat boots—all the better if they're a bright color and have a wedge heel.

★ You're more like Halle: Try boho chic— flowery and flowy dresses, blouses, and pants.

★ You're more like Chloe: Wear a brightly colored tracksuit.

★ Don't forget your huge hoop earrings— the more sparkle the better!

★ In warmer weather, try midriff-baring shirts with high-waisted, wide-legged pants or shorts.

★ Don't go overboard with makeup! Just a little lipstick by day, add dramatic eyes at night.

CHAPTER 9

ON THE GRAM

*I*f there's one recurring dream Chloe and Halle have shared since they were little girls, it's to win a Grammy Award. (Pretty cool dream.) It's not surprising—their first love is music. And the Grammys are the ultimate prize in the music industry. What musician doesn't covet a Grammy? You gotta think that even when musicians say it doesn't matter to them, it must, right?

> Here's the **SCOOP!** The Baileys are pretty open about it. They want one. And, as with all of their goals, the sisters have practiced visualization.

"We'd always put Grammys on our vision boards every year, and I even had a fake Grammy posted on my ceiling," Chloe said.

You may have heard Chloe and Halle use the word *manifestation*. It's something they talk about when they're asked about their process and their goals. What they mean is they like to envision their dreams, that it helps them work for what they want, whether it's an album, a performance, money (yes, they do care about that, too), or the Grammys.

"We totally believe in the power of manifestation, so we've always just closed our eyes and, like, wished and prayed and worked hard," Chloe said.

It was all the hard work that clinched it, but the praying and wishing probably didn't hurt. In December 2018, their Grammy dreams got a little more real with nominations for Best New Artist and Best Urban Contemporary Album for *The Kids Are Alright* at the 61st Grammy Awards. They were pretty shook when they got the news!

"It's so surreal," Chloe said. "This is a big dream come true for us."

They were also invited to sing on the award

show in February 2019. Maybe you were hoping they would sing something from their nominated album. But not this time. They sang the 1972 hit "Where Is the Love" by Roberta Flack and Donny Hathaway, who died in 1979. They paid tribute to Hathaway before they presented the award for Best Rap Album to Cardi B for *Invasion of Privacy*.

The sisters looked amazingly chic in black-tie glam. Chloe wore an asymmetrical black velvet gown with a slit up her thigh, her dreadlocks pulled high on her head. And Halle wore a short black dress with fanned shoulders, her dreadlocks pulled back in a bun.

Their rendition of the song is beautiful—their harmonies perfectly blended. And there's something else to take note of: The performance demonstrates that they're really adults now. The vocals, the sophisticated evening wear, their poise. All of the little-girl stuff was gone—they oozed glamour.

In the end, they didn't win either Grammy. Best Urban Contemporary Album went to *Everything*

Is Love by the Carters (as in Jay-Z and Beyoncé). The Best New Artist award went to Dua Lipa.

It was a night of highs and lows. The losses had to be tough. Artists always say it was an honor to be nominated. So true. But it's still got to sting a bit.

Never fear. When it comes to Chloe and Halle Bailey, there is always something big just around the corner. And 2019 would not disappoint.

SCOOP! FACT

Chloe says she was obsessed with becoming a Broadway star when she was little because it had everything she liked "fused together." Maybe someday she'll win a Tony!

WHAT SHOULD CHLOE AND HALLE DO NEXT?

The sisters have a lot of their dreams covered. What do *you* think Chloe and Halle should do next?

Who would you like to see Chloe date? _____

_____

Who would you like to see Halle date? _____

_____

What movie would you like to see Chloe star in? _____

_____

If the sisters could star in a Broadway show, which one would you choose for them? _____

_____

What new instrument should Chloe learn to play? _____

_____

What new instrument should Halle learn to play? _____

_____

Which of the Chloe x Halle songs should be nominated
for a Grammy? _____

_____

_____

Which clothing line would you like to see the sisters
model for? _____

Should they create their own clothing line? What would
you call it? _____

_____

Who are you more like? Chloe or Halle? _____

_____

CHAPTER 10

UNDER THE SEA

*W*ere you cheering when Halle was named the next Ariel? You weren't alone! But a lot of Halle's supporters also felt they had to come to her defense. Clearly there are still people out there who thought a black woman shouldn't play the Little Mermaid.

First off, let's get something straight: *The Little Mermaid*'s Ariel is a fictional character. She's a MERMAID. Not a person. She's not based on a real-life historical figure. Until now, she's been a cartoon, a drawing that came from someone's imagination, based on a character in a story.

You know all this already, but not everybody gets it.

#NotMyAriel trended on Twitter. It couldn't

have felt good to see that or hear the critics. Haters will be haters. But the always-positive Halle was having none of it.

"I feel like I'm dreaming," she told a *Variety* reporter who asked about the controversy. "I don't pay attention to the negativity. I just feel like this role was something bigger than me and greater, and it's going to be beautiful."

Jodi Benson, the voice of the Disney-animated Ariel, showed up for Halle. "I think that the spirit of a character is what really matters. What you bring to the table in a character as far as their heart, and their spirit, is what really counts." Amen to that.

The Disney-owned Freeform network wrote an open letter to the "poor unfortunate souls" on social media (high-level trolling). "So after all this is said and done, and you still cannot get past the idea that choosing the incredible, sensational, highly talented, gorgeous Halle Bailey is anything other than the INSPIRED casting that it is because she 'doesn't look like the cartoon one,' oh boy, do I have some news for you," Freeform wrote. "About you." Nicely done, Freeform!

But enough about that. You want to know more about the movie to be directed by Rob Marshall, whose credits also include *Mary Poppins Returns* and *Into the Woods*.

Here's the SCOOP! The live-action *Little Mermaid* is going to boast a star-studded cast. As of this writing, it looks like Melissa McCarthy is slated to play the villain Ursula. She will be hilariously evil.

Awkwafina is in talks to play Scuttle the seagull, and Jacob Tremblay could be Ariel's best friend, Flounder the fish. Word on the street is that Javier Bardem is likely to play Ariel's overbearing father, King Triton. And hold on—what about the prince, you ask? Harry Styles was in talks for that important role, but he ultimately passed, so we'll just have to keep waiting to know who will play charming Prince Eric!

The music should be amazing! The score's original composer, Alan Menken, is teaming up with the fabulous Lin-Manuel Miranda for the new score. It's going to include your favorites, plus some additional songs. And with Halle's vocals at the helm, there's no way they can miss.

Here's why Halle is going to slay in this role:

1. Her VOICE! 'Nuff said.
2. Acting chops earned on two seasons of *Grown-ish*.
3. She's drop-dead gorgeous! Forget the red hair. Halle's dreads are more than sea-worthy.
4. Halle and Ariel share a dreaminess—positivity and kindness, too.
5. She'll look amazing in a mermaid tail!

With their soaring vocals, some people have called her and Chloe sirens. (Could Chloe be cast as one of Ariel's sisters?) It's a term used sometimes in music. In Greek mythology, the sirens were dangerous creatures who lured sailors with their enchanting voices, causing them to become ship-wrecked. Halle, dangerous? Depends on how you define that. Her voice is definitely enchanting and more than up to the task. Plus, nobody embodies the spirit of Ariel more than Halle. Brave, loyal, talented, adventurous, and kind—some of the first words that come to mind when you think of the Little Mermaid. (Sound familiar?) She dreamed of being human. The human, Halle, once dreamed of stardom. But she's going to have to find some new dreams, because all of the old ones are coming true.

SCOOP! FACT

When she found out she had the role of Ariel, Halle simply tweeted, "Dream come true," and posted it on Instagram with the now-famous drawing of a black Ariel by artist Dylan Bonner. You've got to wonder if she had a vision board for that, too.

Maybe Chloe x Halle will finally get that Grammy, or maybe they'll write a Broadway show score together. Chloe could star in a feature-length film. Who knows what else they'll do? They probably could conquer anything they set out to do. All they'll need is a little vision and commitment. And you know how that story goes!

SCOOP! QUIZ

HOW WELL DO YOU REMEMBER
THE LITTLE MERMAID?

It may have been a while since you've watched it, but chances are this Disney classic is embedded in your brain for good.

1. Who are Ursula's sidekicks? _____

_____

2. What is the prince's first name? _____

3. Can you name Ariel's six sisters? (Okay—how about one or two?) _____

_____

4. Is "Part of Your World" or "A Whole New World" from *The Little Mermaid?* _____

5. What song does Chef Louis sing? _____

6. Who wrote the score for *The Little Mermaid*? _____

_____

7. Who wrote the original story "The Little Mermaid"?

_____

8. What's the name of the prince's servant? _____

9. What's a snarfblat? _____

10. What's a dinglehopper, and for an extra point, what's it used for? _____

_____

SCORING:

1–4 correct answers: Landlubber

5–7 correct answers: Seagull

8–10 correct answers: Mermaid!

SCOOP! QUIZ

ARE YOU A TRUE FAN?
THE ULTIMATE CHLOE x HALLE QUIZ

So, you think you know them? Take our quiz to find out if you're really a superfan. (Some of the answers are in this book, but no cheating!)

1. What is Jazlyn and Skyler's last name on *Grown-ish*?

_____

2. What is the title of the theme song from *A Wrinkle in Time*? _____

3. What is Chloe and Halle's little brother's name? _____

_____

4. Which Grammy Awards were Chloe x Halle nominated for? _____

5. What film star tweeted, "Halles get it DONE" after Halle got the role of Ariel? _____

_____

6. At what major sporting event did Chloe x Halle sing "America the Beautiful"? _____

_____

7. Where were Chloe and Halle born? _____

_____

8. What "hot" exercise do Chloe and Halle do to stay fit?

_____

9. How many tracks are on their *The Kids Are Alright* album? _____

10. Where were the Baileys when they found out they'd be on the *Ellen* show? _____

_____

11. Who's their favorite First Lady? _____

_____

12. What's Chloe's astrological sign? _____

13. What's Halle's astrological sign? _____

14. What was on the door of their Atlanta house the last day they lived there? _____

15. Which sister likes to read thrillers? _____

16. What are the sisters' parents' names? _____

_____

17. What kind of software do Chloe x Halle use to make music? _____

18. "Soul" is the name of an instrument one of the sisters plays. What is it? _____

19. What song did Chloe x Halle sing at the Grammy Awards? _____

_____

20. Did Chloe go to prom? _____

··
SCORING:

1–5 correct answers: Seriously?

6–10 correct answers: Keep reading

11–15 correct answers: You'd feel at home with the Baileys

16–20 correct answers: Congrats! You're a Chloe x Halle superfan!
··

WRITE YOUR OWN SCOOP!

Write down your three favorite songs by Chloe x Halle. What do you like about each?

1 _____

_____

_____

2 _____

_____

_____

3 _____

_____

_____

Write down your three favorite lyrics from three different songs by Chloe x Halle.

1 _____

_____

_____

_____

2 _____

_____

_____

_____

3 _____

_____

_____

_____

What do you think each lyric means?

1

_____

_____

_____

_____

2

_____

_____

_____

_____

3

_____

_____

_____

_____

If you had the chance to meet Chloe x Halle, what are three questions you would ask them?

1 _____

_____

_____

2 _____

_____

_____

3 _____

_____

_____

Chloe x Halle are performing their next big concert and they need your help to put together the set list! What ten songs do you want to hear?

1. _____

2. _____

3. _____

4. _____

5. _____

6. _____

7. _____

8. _____

9. _____

10. _____

Now it's the encore song of their set . . . but they bring on a special guest musician! Who do they bring on stage and what song would you want to hear them perform together?

_____

_____

_____

_____

_____

_____

_____

ANSWER KEY

WHO SAID IT?

Answer Key: 1. Chloe, 2. Halle, 3. Chloe, 4. Halle, 5. Halle, 6. Chloe, 7. Chloe, 8. Halle, 9. Chloe, 10. Halle

HOW WELL DO YOU KNOW BEYONCÉ?

Answer Key: 1. Giselle, 2. Houston, Texas, 3. Destiny's Child, 4. *Dangerously in Love*, 5. *Lemonade*, 6. Solange Knowles, 7. Blue Ivy Carter, 8. Rumi and Sir, 9. Sasha Fierce, 10. Nala

WHO'S WHO?

Answer Key: 1. Zoey Johnson—Yara Shahidi, 2. Luca—Luka Sabbat, 3. Jazlyn Forster—Chloe Bailey, 4. Nomi Segal—Emily Arlook, 5. Aaron Jackson—Trevor Jackson, 6. Skyler Forster—Halle Bailey, 7. Ana Torres—Francia Raisa, 8. Vivek Shah—Jordan Buhat

HOW WELL DO YOU KNOW THE ALBUM?

Answer Key: 1. "Grown," 2. "Fake," 3. "Hello Friend," 4. "Cool People," 5. "If God Spoke," 6. "Drop," 7. "The Kids Are Alright," 8. "Happy Without Me"

HOW WELL DO YOU REMEMBER *THE LITTLE MERMAID*?

Answer Key: 1. Flotsam and Jetsam,
2. Eric, 3. Aquata, Andrina, Arista, Attina,
Adella, Alana, 4. "Part of Your World,"
5. "Les Poissons," 6. Alan Menken, 7. Hans
Christian Andersen, 8. Grimsby, 9. A pipe,
10. A fork—for combing hair

ARE YOU A TRUE FAN?

Answer Key: 1. Forster, 2. "Warrior,"
3. Branson, 4. Best New Artists and Best Urban
Contemporary Album, 5. Halle Berry, 6. Super
Bowl LIII, 7. Atlanta, 8. Hot yoga, 9. Eighteen,
10. A supermarket, 11. Michelle Obama,
12. Cancer, 13. Aries, 14. A grasshopper,
15. Chloe, 16. Courtney and Doug, 17. Logic Pro
X and Ableton, 18. An acoustic guitar,
19. "Where Is the Love," 20. Yes

HELP US PICK THE
NEXT ISSUE OF

HERE'S HOW TO VOTE:

Go to

www.ReadScoop.com

**to cast your vote for
who we should
SCOOP! next.**